NEAR THE

To the Downtrodden

NEAR THE BONE

ARROW BOOKS

Arrow Books Limited
20 Vauxhall Bridge Road, London SW1V 2SA

An imprint of Random Century Group

London Melbourne Sydney Auckland Johannesburg
and agencies throughout the world

First published by Arrow 1990

© 1990 by Ralph Steadman

Printed and bound in Great Britain by
Courier International Ltd, Tiptree, Essex

ISBN 0 09 973520 2

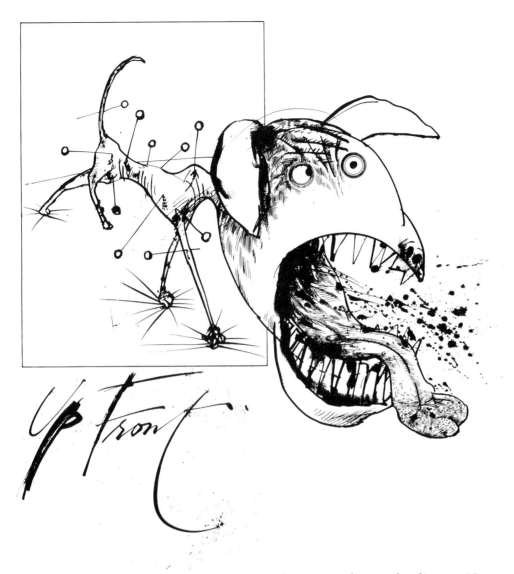

Up Front

I'm not in the least surprised that anyone who owns a dog needs a licence. Never mind one licence, they need three: one for the dog, one for the owner, and one for both of them.

Our streets are fraught with danger at every step. Crowds of apprehensive pedestrians tiptoe along the pavements of our towns and cities in a vain attempt to keep their shoes clean. Decent citizens spend sleepless nights listening to the chilling howls of locked-out Baskerville hounds. Troubled mothers turn back for home rather than subject their infant children to the quivering copulation of love-locked mongrels outside the local supermarket. To visit friends becomes a terrifying ordeal: the moment the front door opens, an unsuspecting visitor is confronted by a slobbering set of ivory-white molars inside a flea-bitten ball of flesh and fluff, leaping toward his face. Millions of honest people, through clever advertising, are led to believe that a can containing a pound of some grisly-looking substance promotes active life and a shiny coat more than a grislier-looking substance out of another can, which an overfed dog rejects under the careful guidance of an expert dog breeder.

The love, affection, and money invested in these pampered beasts brings sighs of despair from welfare workers and members of the NSPCC, who could carry out ninety-eight per cent of their work for neglected children on one-fifth of the revenue gleaned from these campaigns.

But we live in a world of animal lovers and even I find myself at times harbouring a soft spot for dogs. It's something about their eyes, which gaze up at you with such trusting abandon. They bring a lump to my throat and arrest the leg I draw back to kick the swine from here to kingdom come, particularly the little ones – those smooth-coated, yapping, ratlike creatures who really believe that their owner's shit-covered backyard is the whole world, and anyone venturing within ten yards of its perimeters is a green-horned threat from outer space who should be bitten to death.

But I bear no malice. Goodness me, no! How can I? I am blessed with an opportunity to draw it all out of my soul and on to paper. To purge, page by page, the festering source of all resentment. To transform my smoldering heap of loathsome thoughts into a feast of pure delight, I am giving to the world the only decent alternative view of dogs in its entire history. I am offering a sense of proportion; and to those of us who do not share that blind love common to all dog owners, I offer a refuge: the sure knowledge that each of us is not alone, that tyranny and oppression serve only to strike a chord of unity among us, the downtrodden; or rather, we who tread in it. To carry this book with you wherever you go is to carry the cross of protection against the Draculas of our streets, whose 'pets' are no less than the very hounds of hell. Hold this book up against any of them and watch them cower away to drivel and whimper in corners.

Good Luck

Ralph STEADman

FOREWORD

Since I wrote that embittered foreword to *A Leg in the Wind*, the earlier edition of this guide to dog appreciation, I have become the uncertain owner of, and maintenance man to, a dog of my own or, rather, her own – my daughter Sadie actually owns the creature.

Sadie named it Flop because, peculiar to the breed – Flop's a Border Collie – it has a habit of flopping down, chin on floor, looking appealingly and attentively over its eyelids.

The subject of Flop's attention... is me, the centre of her universe, the one who can do no wrong, the masterly voice of reason and control. I did not try to be the one. I became it. Perhaps it was my authoritative manner, or the way I wretched and screamed abuse at the whimpering ball of guilt each morning as I scooped up the pre-house-training mess in a copy of Ruby's *Daily Mail* in those early days. Ruby is my mother-in-law.

We stopped buying newspapers ourselves when we realised that the state of the world wasn't improving, and worse, it was simply repeating itself in colour, ad nauseum. I'm afraid I occasionally had to tell Ruby that her *Mail* hadn't come on that particular day.

She has never liked Flop. No, that's not fair. She will tolerate it as she tolerates me, but she will never let it touch her and now it never does. Me neither. They understand each other, and have what I would call an ideal relationship. Their boundaries are marked and inviolable. In case you are wondering, Ruby and I occasionally have to kiss – when she goes away for a longish period – and when she comes back. No more or less than any good mother and son-in-law. However, I digress.

Flop has in many ways changed my attitude towards dogs and I have become more than tolerant. I am now the one who has to try to explain to the postman why she bit him.

'Look,' I say, 'I'm really sorry about this and I understand your anger and concern, but I can't say *why* she bit you. Maybe she just wants to herd you with the rest of the flock. She does exactly the same with her sheep. Nips them on the ankles, just like that. Now, if *I* had bitten you, I could tell you exactly why.'

Recently I met an animal psychiatrist, Peter Neville, while making a film about dogs. He has helped me to cure Flop, or at least divert her attention with the help of a rape alarm. Pure logic. I think she now associates biting postmen with rape, which goes against her natural sense of right and wrong.

I am still intolerant of people. *We* are to blame for our animal's neurotic behaviour. Peter actually treats the people, though they are not fully aware of this. It is, incidentally, a much cheaper way of getting yourself psychoanalysed, and he can pinpoint your problem in the begging position. You don't have to lie down. He kindly offered to do me, and I proudly publish his findings in this book. It may be of some comfort to you.

I think the book is now more or less comprehensive, honed and added to over the years, since its first appearance in 1970. I am shocked by much of it but would not exclude it, for my more youthful outbursts are imbued with the ring of crude truth. I consider this to be a hedge against complacency.

I have not completely sold out to those who claim to be dog-lovers, but I understand them better now. They are a breed like any other and victim to their own inherant peculiarities. No, I blame the breeders. The over-breeders and the in-breeders, the real instigators of animal misery, merely in business to reflect and flatter our own thoughtless roles. I have seen their results in overcrowded destitute-dogs' homes.

Dogs never complain and will adore anyone, given half a chance. If you kick them they take the blame willingly, and if you dye them pink they will never realise. They are colour blind. If you buy them to go with the furniture and then change your colour scheme, they won't understand your change of heart. If you do get a dog for any reason, then the reason must include a simple loving one – the only kind the creature will understand. It won't understand, neither will it complain when you drop it off on some lonely road, sometime in early January when you've just taken down the Christmas decorations. If it is lucky enough to get picked up then it has seven days to live unless you have another change of heart and claim it back.

Don't buy from a breeder if you can bear to go to a dogs' home and choose a wretched sight, with big eyes, in a cage. At least you will take it for the right reasons and help to reduce the load on those good folk who care for them.

The truth of the matter, I suspect, is somewhere between the contradictions this new foreword creates. I am still not a dog lover, but I would defend the basic right of any creature against the thoughtless bestiality of man. I must be going soft.

Ralph Steadman

13 Feb. 1990

Choosing the SONOFABITCH

CHOOSE YOUR PUPPY AT A REPUTABLE BREEDERS...

MAKING THE FINAL CHOICE:
THE SECRET IS — LET THE **DOG** COME TO YOU.
DONT MAKE A LUNGE FOR THE FIRST ONE THAT CLAPS EYES ON YOU
TALK TO THEM ALL IN A **LOW** FRIENDLY VOICE. THE DOG
FOR YOU WILL CHOOSE **YOU**, ALL BY ITSELF. AVOID A DOG
WHO RETREATS. IT IS SHOWING SIGNS OF FEAR AND ANXIETY. YOU
ARE TRIGGERING ITS PARTICULAR ANXIETY SYNDROME. BEWARE! THESE
POOR CREATURES ARE OFTEN "SPECIAL
OFFERS" OR "DOG OF THE MONTH"
BARGAINS. UNLESS YOU
HAVE THE COMPASSION
OF **ST. FRANCIS** OF
ASSISI — FORGET
IT! (BUT WHO
KNOWS — YOU MAY BE
THE FRUSTRATED MOTHER
THERESA OF THE DOG
WORLD LOOKING FOR
A CAUSE).

DISCIPLINE

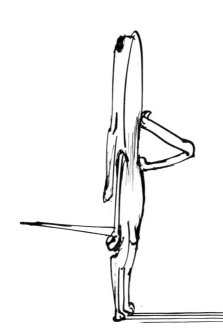

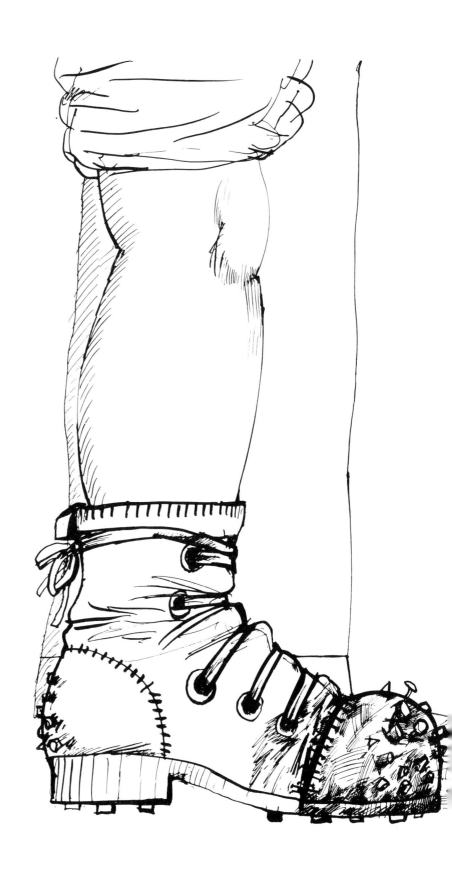

HOW TO TREAT YOUR DOG AND DISCIPLINE HIM. 1

DON'T BE FOOLED BY THE LOOK — HE'S HOPING YOU WILL SAY "THERE, THERE, DON'T DO IT AGAIN" SO THAT HE CAN DO IT AGAIN —— PUT THE *BOOT IN RIGHT AWAY; DON'T HESITATE FOR A MOMENT!

* CORRECTIVE BOOTS CAN BE OBTAINED FROM ALL GOOD PET SHOPS — RIGHT OR LEFT FEET.

HOW TO TREAT YOUR DOG AND DISCIPLINE ~~HIM~~ IT: 2
TEACHING YOUR DOG TO TAKE A BATH MAY NEED MORE
RESTRAINT THAN YOU HAVE HANDS FOR. BATH CLAMPS
ARE A MUST, OTHERWISE YOU'LL GET THE BATH AND
THE DOG WILL PUT THE REST OF THE WATER ON YOUR
WALL.

HOW TO DISCIPLINE YOUR DOG. 3

WAIT UNTIL YOUR DOG IS IN THE BEGGING POSITION THEN SMARTLY DROP A PICKLE DOWN HIS OPEN GULLET — HE'LL NEVER BEG AGAIN.

HOW TO TREAT YOUR DOG AND DISCIPLINE HIM — 4

IT'S NOT ON TO TEACH YOUR DOG ROAD SENSE.
ROAD USERS DONT HAVE ANY THEMSELVES.
GIVE YOUR DOG THE BENEFIT OF THE DOUBT. EVEN
STUPID DOGS WILL LEARN HOW TO AVOID THE HARD
HARD KNOCKS—EVENTUALLY...

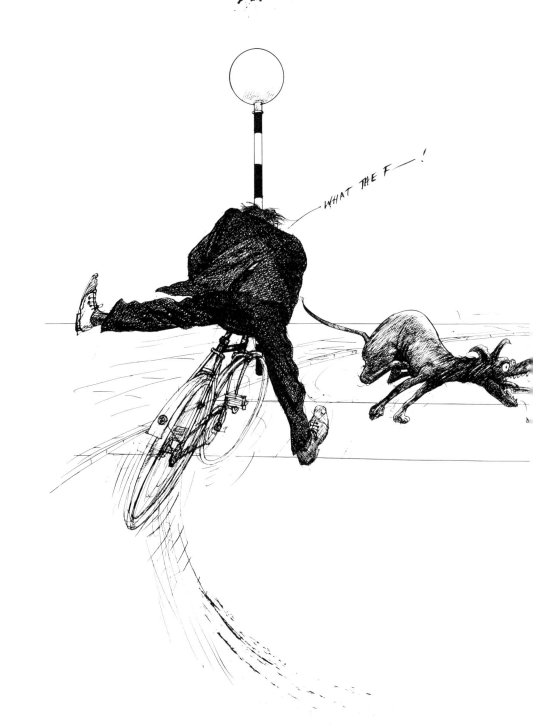

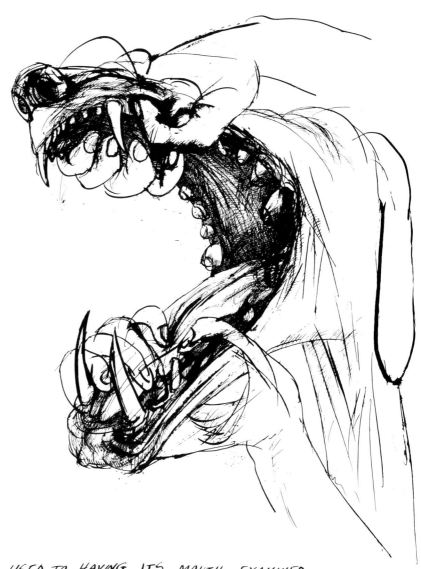

GET **YOUR** DOG USED TO HAVING ITS MOUTH EXAMINED.
<u>DENTAL EXAMINATION POSTS</u> ARE THOROUGHLY
RECOMMENDED.
    OPEN ITS MOUTH IN A MASTERLY FASHION.
DONT BE TIMID. HE WONT BITE YOU. BUT YOU'LL
BE HORRIFIED! YOU AND I BRUSH OUR TEETH THREE
TIMES A DAY AFTER MEALS — THEY DONT........

HOW TO **TREAT** YOUR **DOG** AND DISCIPLINE HIM — **6.** EVERYONE KNOWS THAT THERE IS NOTHING MORE DISGUSTING THAN TO DISCOVER THAT YOUR CHILD HAS FOU**ND** ONE OF FIDO'S MISTAKES IN THE LIVING ROOM, AND THEY USUALLY DO. THE SOONER YOUR DOG IS HOUSE-TRAINED THE BETTER AND SAFER FOR **ALL.** —— WHILST SCOLDING YOUR DOG FIERCELY RUB YOUR CHILD'S NOSE IN IT RIGHT AWAY. IF DOGS ARE AS F—— INTELLIGENT AS **WE** OWNERS GIVE THEM CREDIT FOR , THEY'LL CATCH ON, WON'T THEY ?

HOW TO TREAT YOUR DOG AND DISCIPLINE HIM—7

EXERCISING YOUR DOG NEED NOT BE THE TIME-
CONSUMING-OCCUPATION OWNERS MAKE IT OUT TO BE.....

LEG IN A HIGH WIND

signs to WATCH FOR.

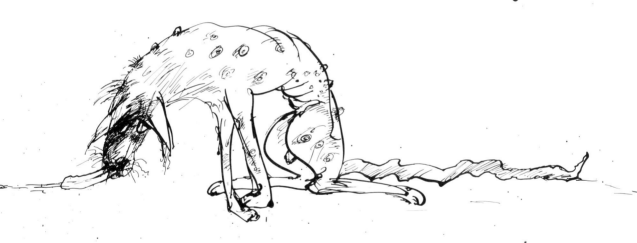

SIGNS TO WATCH FOR: 1

A BITCH ON HEAT DEMANDS CONSTANT OBSERVATION IF A MISALLIANCE IS TO BE AVOIDED. OBEDIENCE COUNTS FOR NOTHING WHEN A BITCH FALLS VICTIM TO ITS OWN SEXUAL INSTINCTS. VETERINARY CHLOROPHYLL, DEODORIZING FLUID AND AEROSOL SCENT MASKS WORK, UP TO A POINT BUT THE ONLY SURE WAY IS TO CUT OFF THE HIND LEGS (SEE DOTTED LINE).

SIGNS TO WATCH FOR: 2

WHEN A DOG IS HUNGRY THE REASON IS
OFTEN NOT SIMPLY LAC<u>K</u> OF **FOOD** — BUT
VARIETY.
    IF HE ▅▅▅▅▅ CHEWS HIS LEG OFF
AND BRINGS IT TO YOU, HE MAY BE TRYING
  TO TELL YOU THAT HE HAS HAD ENOUGH OF THE
SAME OLD THING.

        IF AFTER REMEDIAL ACTION THE
        CONDITION <u>STILL</u> PERSISTS AND
        HE CHEWS ANOTHER LEG OFF, THEN
      HE PROBABLY WANTS **WHEELS**

SIGNS TO WATCH FOR: 3

IF A DOG GOES OFF ITS FOOD OR VOMITS, COUGHS, DISCHARGES FROM THE EYES; SEEMS LETHARGIC OR SIMPLY LIES DOWN AND STOPS BREATHING, IMMEDIATE ACTION IS NECESSARY. DON'T WAIT FOR THE VET. HE IS INVARIABLY OVERWORKED, SICK LIKE YOUR DOG, OR INVOLVED IN A ROAD ACCIDENT ON HIS WAY OVER.

ARTIFICIAL RESPIRATION SHOULD BE ATTEMPTED IF A SWIFT KICK IN THE RIBS DOESN'T DO THE TRICK.

THE OLD FASHIONED METHOD OF RHYTHMIC PRESSURE TO THE RIB CAGE CAN WORK, BUT IN THE CASE OF SMALL DOGS, MOUTH TO MOUTH RESUSCITATION IS VERY POPULAR WITH MODERN DOG OWNERS

THIS IS **NOT** ADVISABLE WITH BIG DOGS.
WAIT FOR THE **VET**. HE GETS PAID FOR IT.

SIGNS TO WATCH FOR: 4

LOVE AND ATTENTION: YOU MAY HAVE PICKED THE WRONG DOG — BUT EVEN A WRONG DOG NEEDS A LITTLE LOVE. YOU OWE IT TO HIM TO TRY......

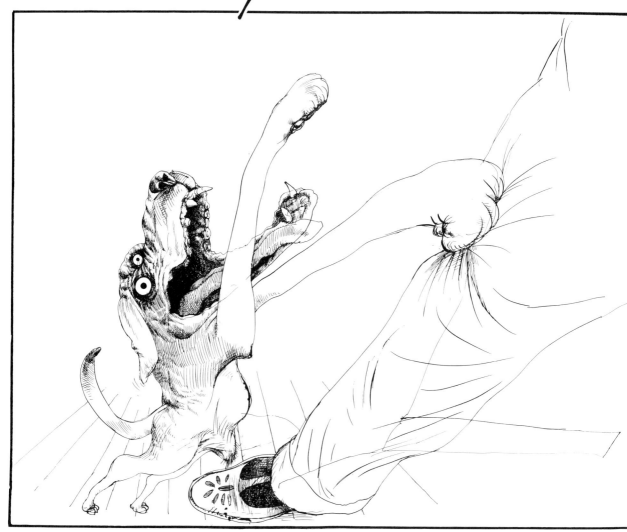

SIGNS TO WATCH FOR: 5

'THAT LOOK' IS A DOG'S STRONGEST
WEAPON, AND THE DOG KNOWS IT.
THE SWINE WILL MELT YOU
MERCILESSLY WITH JUNGLE CUNNING
TO GET WHAT IT WANTS. HOWEVER
YOU DEAL WITH IT THE LOOK
PREVAILS. ONLY IN A DRAWING CAN
YOU OBLITERATE IT — AND EVEN
THEN IT WHIMPERS THROUGH.
SO BEWARE OF IT — AND THE
FIRST SIGN — SHOVE THE BUGGER
IN THE WOODSHED!

SIGNS TO WATCH FOR: 6

TWO-DOG FAMILIES DESERVE TO SUFFER
THIS KIND OF PUBLIC DISPLAY. IT IS USUALLY
A SIGN THAT THE WHOLE DAMN FAMILY DOESN'T
KNOW WHETHER IT IS COMING OR GOING.

SIGNS TO WATCH FOR: 7

THIS IS A PERFECTLY NATURAL FAMILIARISATION
RITUAL. PEOPLE DO EXACTLY THE SAME WITH A
LITTLE MORE SUBTLETY. IF IT PERSISTS THOUGH,
GO SEE THE VET — OR A DOCTOR/PSYCHIATRIST IN
YOUR CASE. A VET HAS AT LEAST TEN DIFFERENT
BRANDS OF OZONE FRIENDLY PERFUME SPRAYS TO MAKE
YOUR DOG'S BUM SMELL LIKE PARADISE. AND
YOU? TRY BOOTS. THEY SELL ANYTHING THESE
DAYS.— EXCEPT ADVICE.

TAKING A DOG'S TEMPERATURE:

NOBODY. WOULD BE FOOLISH ENOUGH TO PRETEND
THAT SUCH A PROCEDURE IS A DODDLE. A DOG'S
TEMPERATURE IS TAKEN RECTALLY. TRY TO IMAGINE YOURSELF
CORNERED BY SOMEONE WHOM YOU THOUGHT WAS A FRIEND, HOLDING A
LONG GLASS TUBE FULL OF MERCURY AND SMEARED WITH VASELINE, TELLING
YOU IN CHINESE THAT THEY ARE GOING TO STICK IT UP YOUR BACKSIDE—
FOR NO APPARENT REASON. . . .

LIKE ME

—LIKE MY DOG

Man leading
his blind dog specially
bought for him by ~~she did~~ kindly donations.

A PRIZE-WINNING BITCH.

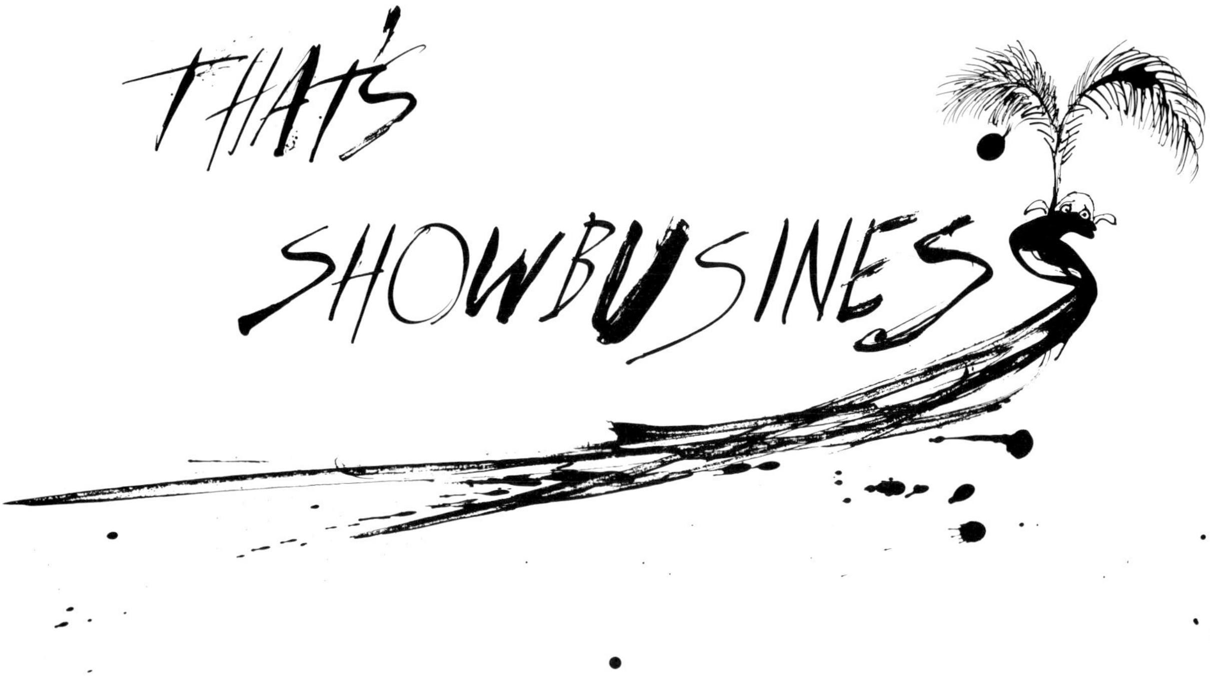
THAT'S
SHOWBUSINESS

Style your PEKE
from this

to this !

IN ALL PURSUITS,
IN ALL AREAS OF HUMAN
ENDEAVOUR, THERE ARE
THOSE WHO WILL SETTLE
FOR NOTHING LESS THAN
PERFECTION.....

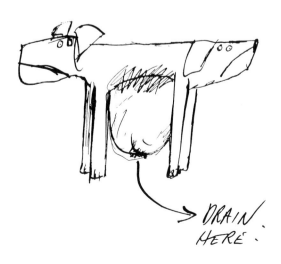

→ DRAIN
HERE

.... In our modern world of lowered standards and the cult of the **3rd** rate, it is the firm resolve of *A DEDICATED PAWFUL*...

Gable End

EARS TOO SHORT

GAY TWITCH.

BREECH LOADING REVERSIBLE

FLASH POINT II (GALVANISE EARS!)

RE:—
Veronica Crewe-Connolly
Called — is
her dog ready yet.?
Phone her please.
on HORSEMAN'S END 249.

LESS
CHIN

OFF!

6"

SHAVE ACROSS BOTTOM.

.... IN THE DOG WORLD TO 'REVERSE THAT TREND,
AND WORK TIRELESSLY TO CREATE
THE PERFECT BEAST.....

.....; A SERVILE RACE, NO LESS.

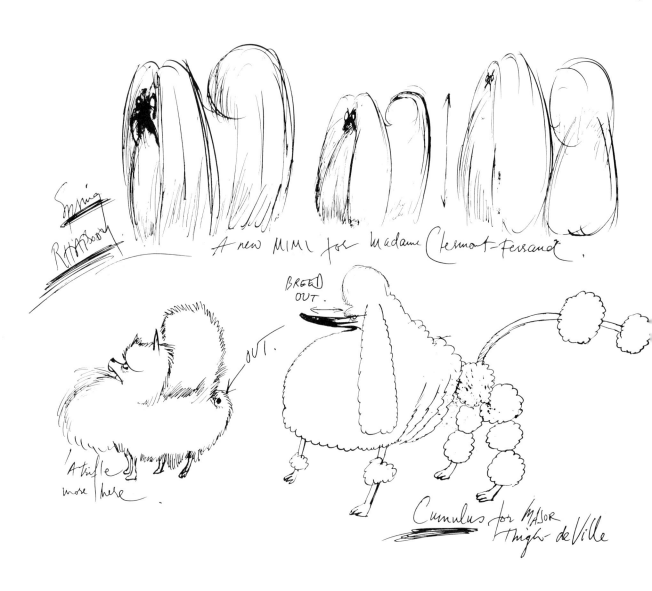

Spring
Rhapsody

A new MIMI for Madame Clermont-Ferrand.

BREED
OUT.

OUT.

A trifle
more here

Cumulus for MAJOR
Thigh-de Ville

THE CUSTODIANS OF THESE MODISHLY STYLED CREATURES ARE OUR BULWARKS AGAINST NATURE'S FUMBLING COMMONPLACE.

AT THE END OF THE DAY....

.....THEY ASK FOR NOTHING BUT THE SIMPLE KNOWLEDGE THAT THEY CAN HOLD THEIR TAILS UP HIGH AND BE SURE THAT TRUE BREEDING WILL BE RECOGNIZED FOR WHAT IT DOES ....

BUSINESS MATTERS

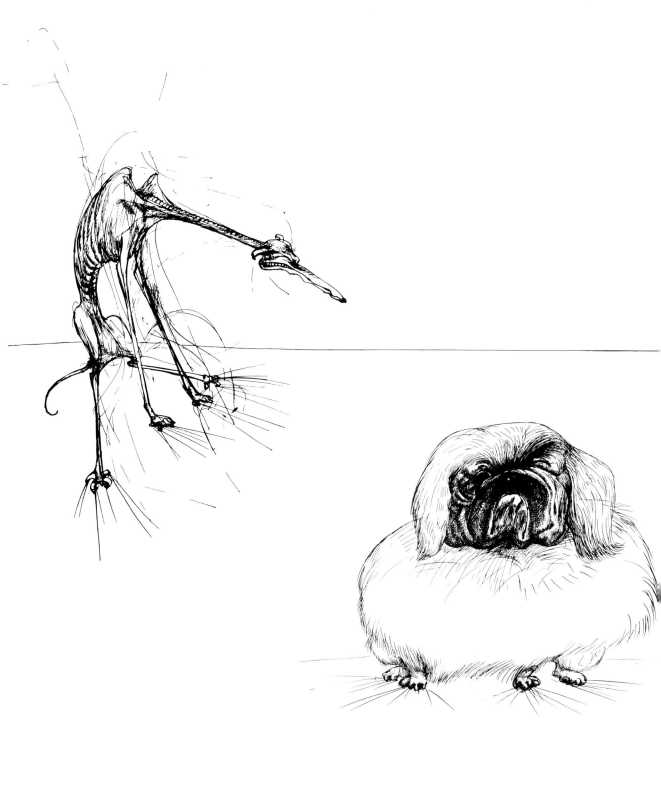

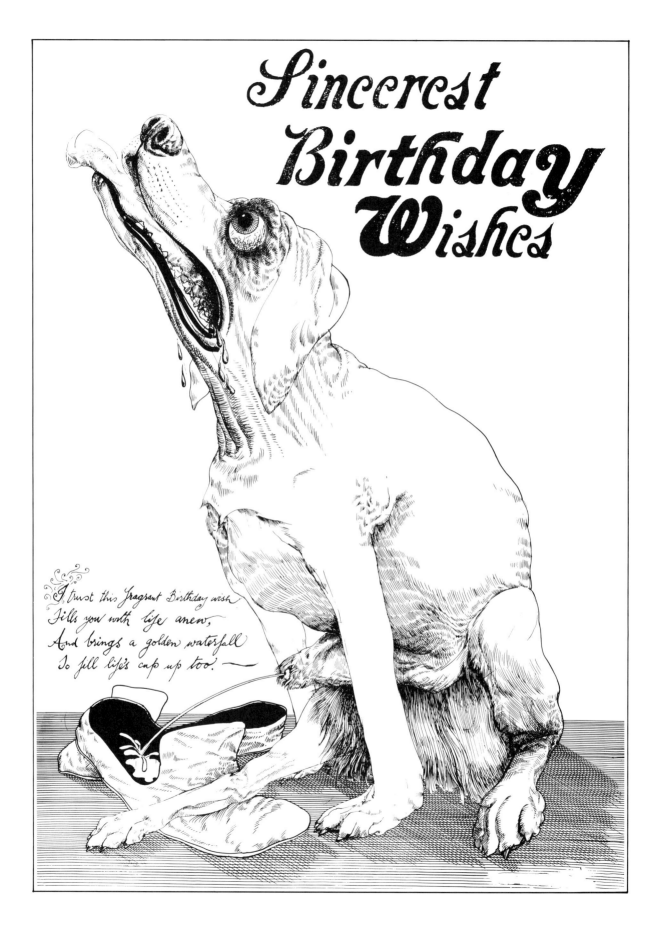

THE OBESITY CLINIC

OWNER WITH FAT WHIPPET.

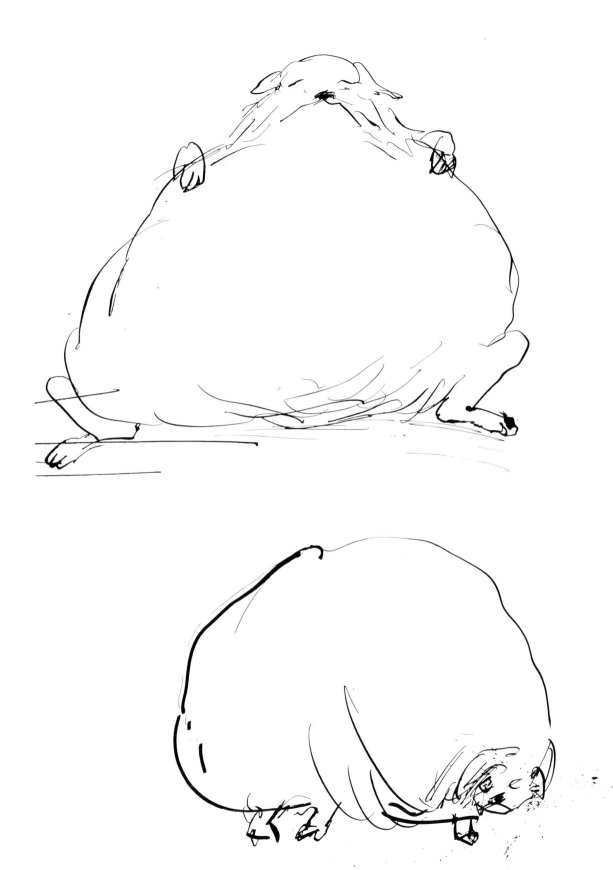

Lotus.
the overweight WHIPPET.

Van

THE ONLY SAFE ROTTWEILER
IS A FAT ROTTWEILER
— PROVIDED YOU CAN RUN VERY FAST

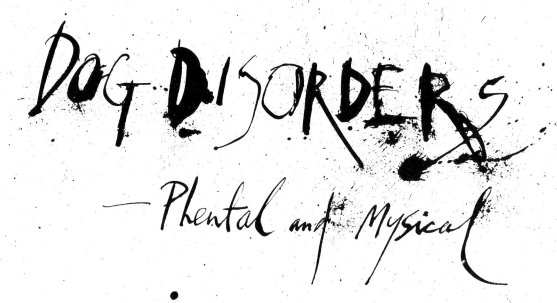

DOG DISORDERS
— Phental and Mysical

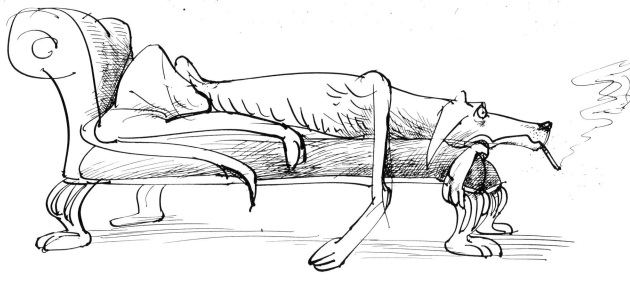

THE DOG WHO PUTS ITS HEAD ON YOUR KNEE PATHETICALLY AND HOLDS ITS STOMACH HAS GOT MORE THAN SIMPLE STOMACH ACHE. IT IS SUFFERING FROM AN IDENTITY CRISIS. IT MAY THINK IT'S A KANGAROO. IT IS INVARIABLY BROUGHT ON BY AN OWNER WITH THE SAME PROBLEM. IF YOU CAN'T PULL YOURSELF TOGETHER THEN AT LEAST TRY PLAYING KANGAROOS WHEN YOU TAKE THE DAILY WALK. HOP ALONG WITH YOUR DOG AT YOUR SIDE. THE DOG WILL FEEL RIDICULOUS AND STOP BEING A KANGAROO TO BECOME SOMETHING ELSE. UNLESS YOU DECIDE WHO **YOU** REALLY ARE THEN THE DOG'S CONDITION IS INCURABLE.

IF YOUR DOG STARTS THE DISTRESSING HABIT OF CHASING ITS OWN TAIL YOU MUST DIVERT ITS ATTENTION BY GETTING IT TO CHASE YOURS. A 'TAIL STICK' IS A GOOD TEMPORARY MEASURE WAGGED SENSITIVELY WITH YOUR INDEX FINGER.

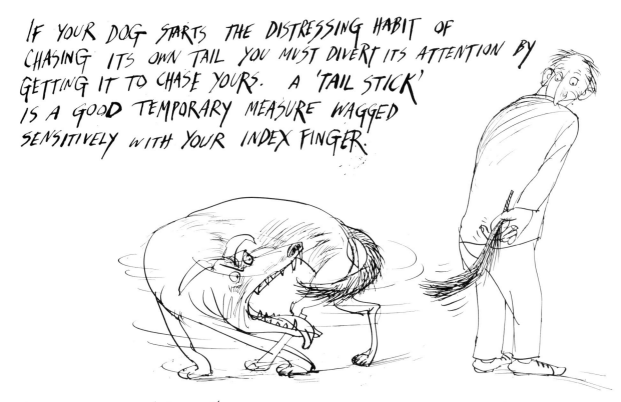

THE BEST SOLUTION HOWEVER IS TO GO THE WHOLE HOG AND INVEST IN A 'TAIL HARNESS'

REAL DOG LOVERS WOULD NOT HESITATE......

.....ALSO AVAILABLE ARE 'EAR HELMETS' AND 'TONGUE GAGS' FOR THE QUINTESSENTIAL DOGGY LOOK. YOU MAY NOT CURE THE DOG BUT HE WILL HAVE THE SATISFACTION OF KNOWING THAT YOU ARE MADDER THAN HE IS.

NOISELESS FLATULENCE CAN BE A REAL
SOCIAL EMBARRASSMENT. AND IS COMMON
IN BIG DOGS. WHOSE DIETS ARE
SUPPLEMENTED IN BULK WITH GRAIN AND
SOYA BEAN PRODUCTS. ONE IS NEVER
SURE OF THE CULPRIT AND THE POOR
OWNER IS BLAMED MORE OFTEN THAN NOT
QUITE UNFAIRLY.

UNFORTUNATELY THE ONLY CURE FOR THIS
CONDITION IS A LONGER LEAD — BUT
FAITHFUL DOGS TEND TO STICK
CLOSE TO THEIR OWNERS ON SUCH
OCCASIONS.

THE HELPLESS BEGGING POSITION IS **NOT** A GOOD SIGN. IT IS USUALLY A DIETARY PROBLEM. THE DOG IS TRYING TO TELL YOU IT IS **NOT** A VEGETARIAN AND NEVER WILL BE. UNTIL DOG FOOD MANUFACTURERS STOP TRYING TO PEDDLE THEIR RIDICULOUS DOGGY-VEG PRODUCTS YOUR PET WILL CONTINUE TO LOOK PATHETIC. YOU **MUST** RESIST THE HIGH-PRESSURE ADVERTISING AND YOUR OWN NEW MORAL STANCE ON EATING MEAT AND GIVE THE DOG A BONE..

FURNITURE CHEWING IS NOT ONLY IRRITATING, BUT IT CAUSES A DOG TO WRETCH AND CHOKE ON THE WEIRD SYNTHETIC FIBRES USED IN MODERN FURNITURE TODAY.

DOGS MUCH PREFER THE OLD HORSE HAIR STUFFING, REAL LEATHER COVERED CHESTERFIELDS, AND THE GOOD SOLID MAHOGANY OF A QUEEN ANNE CHAIR LEG.

IT IS UNFAIR TO EXPECT A DOG TO ADAPT TO THIS NEW FIREPROOF RUBBISH PEOPLE ARE BEING FOOLED INTO BUYING THESE DAYS

A letter from a leading dog psychiatrist to Ralph's owner, Anna Steadman.

19 May 1989

Dear Anna

Re: Ralph – British Bulldog X Welsh mongrel, male

Further to my visit I write to reiterate my advice concerning Ralph's behaviour with specific reference to his slightly dominating character and global territorial marking. In most respects Ralph is very pleasant but has retained many of his early tough characteristics. A born pack leader, Ralph presents many of the traits of a dominant dog, including aloofness manifested by his history as something of a loner, but for the most part you have learned to cope well with him. However, he is still prone to showing occasional outbursts of dominant aggression, barking when frustrated or over-excited indoors and other 'blokish' behaviour. Treatment therefore is aimed at firmly re-establishing your role as top dog and managing the more unpleasant aspects of his otherwise lovable character.

Maintaining your Dominance

While Ralph is now more mellow than when you found him on the streets of south-west London, his aggressive defence of acquired advantage on high vantage points, such as on the sofa, demands that you maintain your height over him at all times. Never give up your advantage by meeting him at eye level and never bend over him, especially when he is working. This may be seen as a challenge and he may growl to warn you away.

Ideally he should not be allowed to sleep on your bed but as detaching him from this established privilege may be dangerous at this stage, at least ensure that you are in bed before allowing him to jump up, and only let him curl up at your feet. Establish your right to his resting areas downstairs by sitting or lying on them frequently in front of him. Never challenge him should he gain the advantage, as he may snap. Instead, bribe him away using food and reward his compliance. Indeed as Ralph is a rather greedy dog you should use food to divert any unwanted behaviour rather than seeking to punish him physically. You have probably avoided being bitten in the past by your wise policy of non-confrontation and this should be continued.

Most important of all however is for you to mimic the behaviour of a high ranking dog yourself so that Ralph perceives you as the pack leader. Try to reject all his demands for attention or efforts to initiate contact for 2-3 weeks to re-define your relationship. Offer affection only at your initiation and for a duration of your choosing and then switch off. He may try harder initially to make you respond to him but resist the big-eyed looks and he will soon learn that life occurs through your intentions, not his.

Block attempts to engage in territorial defence barking (another common behaviour of the high-ranking male) by startling him immediately after a bark using a rape alarm as demonstrated. Use the window of opportunity to take control by enforcing an obedience command, which should be rewarded, and continuing to keep him calm using affection, and perhaps food rewards short term as rewards for silence.

Avoid all competitive games with Ralph, as you know from experience that when excited he is most likely to suffer from sudden mood swings and become aggressive. Also he is strong enough to win at games such as tug-o-war with the bedclothes and may become possessive over the spoils of his victories. Instead, commands such as throw-fetch or 'draw a picture' where he is encouraged to develop his own natural talents.

As with many tough dogs Ralph is especially confident on his home territory and often feels vulnerable away from home in unfamiliar areas. However, do not pander to his desires to stay indoors with you; instead, take him to as wide a variety of places as possible and deliberately introduce him to as many dogs and people as you can find. This will maintain his competence at dealing with change and fuel his dependence on your leadership. Do avoid aggressive dogs, those with indiscriminate toilet problems and those with obsessive owners, as Ralph is predictably aggressive in such circumstances and may put himself and you at risk.

Practise basic obedience training as a regular feature of Ralph's life with you during exercise, in the garden and especially indoors. Be sure to precede all the good things of life such as being let out, affection and especially feeding, by expecting a good response to a simple command such as 'sit' or 'wait'. His annoying occasional selective deafness to the 'come here' command when in his studio kennel should then improve, as a conditioned reaction expecting rewards of food becomes established. Always reward correct responses and never punish relapses. Simply insist and he should become increasingly subordinate and respectful, yet without surrendering any of that strong, inquisitive character.

Control of Territorial Marking and Sexual Behaviour

Most high ranking dogs are prone to roaming in search of bitches, but you are fortunate in that Ralph roams only to the local hostelry, and on a predictable daily basis, to include it and the pathways inbetween as part of his territory. While he is something of a sexy dog you seem to have this under control. He does not exhibit any inappropriate sexual behaviour such as mounting chairs or the legs of visitors as many of his ilk will often do. However, Ralph does frequently mark his territory indoors with his own distinctive splashes and indeed is clearly bent on ensuring that he marks as many walls, and galleries especially, throughout the world. At home you should clean up his efforts using a solution of biological detergent followed by a wipe with alcohol, and try to supervise his access indoors at all times. Should he try to lift a leg, startle him with a jet of water or a sudden noise and then kindly lead him to his studio where it is acceptable for him to mark, as only he has to live with it.

I suspect it is too late with a dog of this age to modify his marking away from home, but as such behaviour arises as part of the normal secondary sexual development of the male and is under the influence of androgens (male hormones), you may find that the behaviour would improve if Ralph were to receive an anti-male hormone injection from your vet. While castration often resolves these problems in the adolescent, it is unlikely to reform Ralph very much as his patterns of marking have become learned rather than being continually hormonally motivated. In any case Ralph, as a slightly overweight, older dog of eight (dog) years, presents something of an increased surgical risk nowadays.

Similarly, it is probably too late to modify Ralph's food-guarding tendencies, though insisting that he sits before eating and offering a less palatable diet may help. His tendency to suffer from gastric upset, wind and weight problems would also diminish under a more bland dietary regime. A lower protein intake may also improve any tendency to be moody or over-reactive.

Finally I would doubt that Ralph's slight alopecia is in any way psychogenic in origin as he is largely a confident and adaptable character in the face of stress. It is probably simply due to age!

I'm sure that Ralph is in exactly the right hands for best improvements and – even if progress is slow in some areas of re-defining his status in your family – that you will nonetheless continue to put up with him. He is, as you say, one of the family now, and euthanasia is unthinkable even if on some days he drives you to distraction. Do call and let me know how treatment progresses after the crucial first 2-3 weeks, or immediately should any serious problems arise.

With best regards,

Yours sincerely

Peter Neville BSc (Hons)
Consultant in Animal Behaviour
Chairman, Association of Pet Behaviour Consultants,
United Kingdom

And so.........

Nail clipping: about once every six months, a truly
therapeutic activity for owners with nervous disorders
of their own

Pedigrees of the WORLD

THE BALI MOUNTAIN DOG
(Kintamani Bali CenoFlebitus.)

Undiscovered pedigree breeds are practically an impossibility in this rarified area of well-documented species. However, occasionally, one can happen upon such a occurrence in the most unexpected places, in my case on the island of BALI, now flawed jewel of the South Pacific.

Although not yet accepted by the International Federation of Cynology, BALI MOUNTAIN DOG must be an indigenous breed common to Bali, the first ever Indonesian pedigree. This is due to the fact that the Rabies Ordnance Act of 1926 kept out all foreign dogs which mainly came from China. Predominantly white with brown tinges in the ears, occasionally black ones emerge, and sometimes spotted black and white. In appearance they look like a cross between a corgi, an Alsatian and a skunk, and it seems to have inherited the skunk's distinctive odour. However, the breed remains essentially 'pure', with its characteristically flea-bitten appearance. The Balinese adore them and on enquiry I was informed that on average a family will eat about one a month.

I look forward to seeing this hearty little creature one day being paraded proudly around the ring at Crufts, fleas an' all; for that is, I would say, an essential part of its rich interbreeding, and a much more wholesome attribute than a flattened nose, and other common pedigree qualities too numerous to mention.

I have come across no other such pure specimens in my travels and therefore this section is complete as far as present records go.

KINTAMANI DOG (BALI FLEBITUS) IN
TYPICAL BALLETIC POSTURE

MOTHER WITH MILK

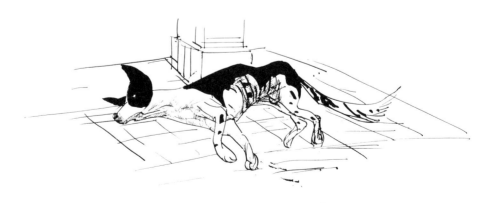

GENERALLY IN APPEARANCE BALI FLEBITUS
IS A CROSS BETWEEN A CORGI, AN
ALSATION AND A SKUNK....

...THEY FREQUENTLY
SLEEP ON THE
STEPS OF
BALINESE
SACRED
TEMPLES......

.....AND HUNGER GIVES THEM THAT QUINTESSENTIAL
BALINESE LOOK.... IF YOU SEE A FAT ONE, IT IS ABOUT
TO BE EATEN

Breeds to Avoid

SOME BREEDS ARE VIRTUALLY UNTRAINABLE. OFTEN FROM FINE PEDIGREE STOCK THEY LURCH ON TWO LEGS, REDOLENT WITH INHERENT TRAITS, DIFFICULT TO CONTROL AND IMPOSSIBLE TO ERADICATE.

AFTER GENERATIONS OF INBREEDING AND PLANNED GENETIC RE-STRUCTURING THESE WRETCHED, MAWKISH MUTANTS CLING DESPERATELY TO THE RARIFIED PERIMETERS OF DOG'S OWN KINGDOM.

Jack the Lad Pinscher

Old English Shortcake

THEY DROOL HEAVILY AND SWEAT WITH ALMOST FEROCIOUS DELIBERATION. DISPLAYING HUMAN TRAITS CONSIDERED BY MANY TO BE APPEALING THEY ATTACH THEMSELVES TO 'LEAD' DOGS AND WALK CEREMONIOUSLY AROUND SHOW RINGS UNDER THE CAREFUL SCRUTINY OF OTHER SIMILAR BREEDS WHO SCRATCH THEIR MARKS OF APPROVAL OR DISDAIN ONTO LARGE SHEETS OF PAPER OF A TYPE OFTEN USED IN THE HOUSE TRAINING OF PUPPIES. THIS RITUAL HAPPENS WITH ALARMING REGULARITY AND IS CONSIDERED BY SOME TO BE AN EXTENSION OF NORMAL TERRITORY MARKING, THOUGH AN UNHEALTHY INSISTENCE ON A CLAIM MANIFESTS ITSELF BY A DEMAND FOR PUBLIC APPROVAL IN THE FORM OF AN AWARDED ROSETTE.

BREEDS OF THIS ~~ONE~~ KIND ARE BEST LEFT TO THOSE WHO CREATE THEM, AND WHO CONSIDER BREEDING IN ANY FORM TO BE A REASON FOR LIVING......

Afghan BLOOMER

Benjalah Basenjis
BOARDMARKER

Boxer BITCH Class

Pomeranian PUSSYDOG

Boozer BEAGle

Dandie Dinmont CLUBHUAHUA

Short-haired PUTTER

Fuzzy BASKERVILLE

Unloved GRIFFON WAGGER

Poppadom POODLE.

DOG'S LIFE

Notes from a Dog's HOME

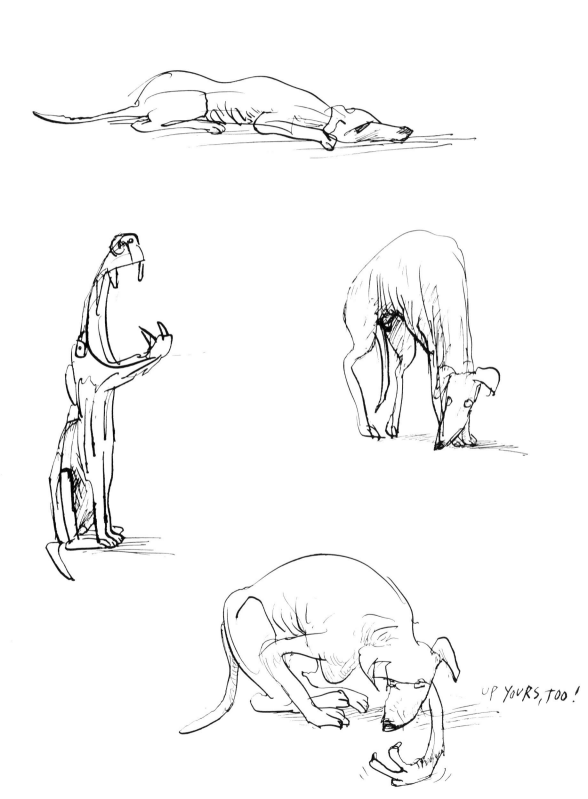

UP YOURS, TOO!

R.I.P

In Championship days......

A week ago....

In Loving memory of
BEDSOCK BOOBOO GHENGIS
KHAN DE CROTCHLICK
Sadly we had to have her
put down

— we'll never
forget you
BEDSOCK.

Why STUFF IT when they SNUFF IT?

GET IT and SET IT IN 24 CARAT SOLID CLEAR PLASTIC!

FANTASTIC!!

THE FLOP FILE.

FLOP driving me to abstraction.....

Working on the principle that you either catch an attitude or you don't, in any given split second, I have tried to convey a few of the various moods of FLOP's character in direct application of black and white.

Sometimes heavily abstracted, or in layman's language, slapped on, the ink has been directed with a certain subliminal response to her constant changes. The ink's own chance happenings on the paper either augment the attitudes in the most unexpected and exciting ways, or add extraneous appendages you either decide to leave or to obliterate. However, the latter usually destroys the spontaneity and to 'fiddle' should be avoided.

Essentially, you apply a blot to the virgin white and seek out the initial observation that guided it. That's your first drawing lesson. If you've got a white dog – that's a whole new ball game. So if you are having trouble with this technique, have your dog put down and get a black one.

All in all FLOP is in there somewhere in various ways, but you can never catch every nuance. There are a million of them....

FLOP is not impressed.

FLOP AT WORK   Ralph Steadman

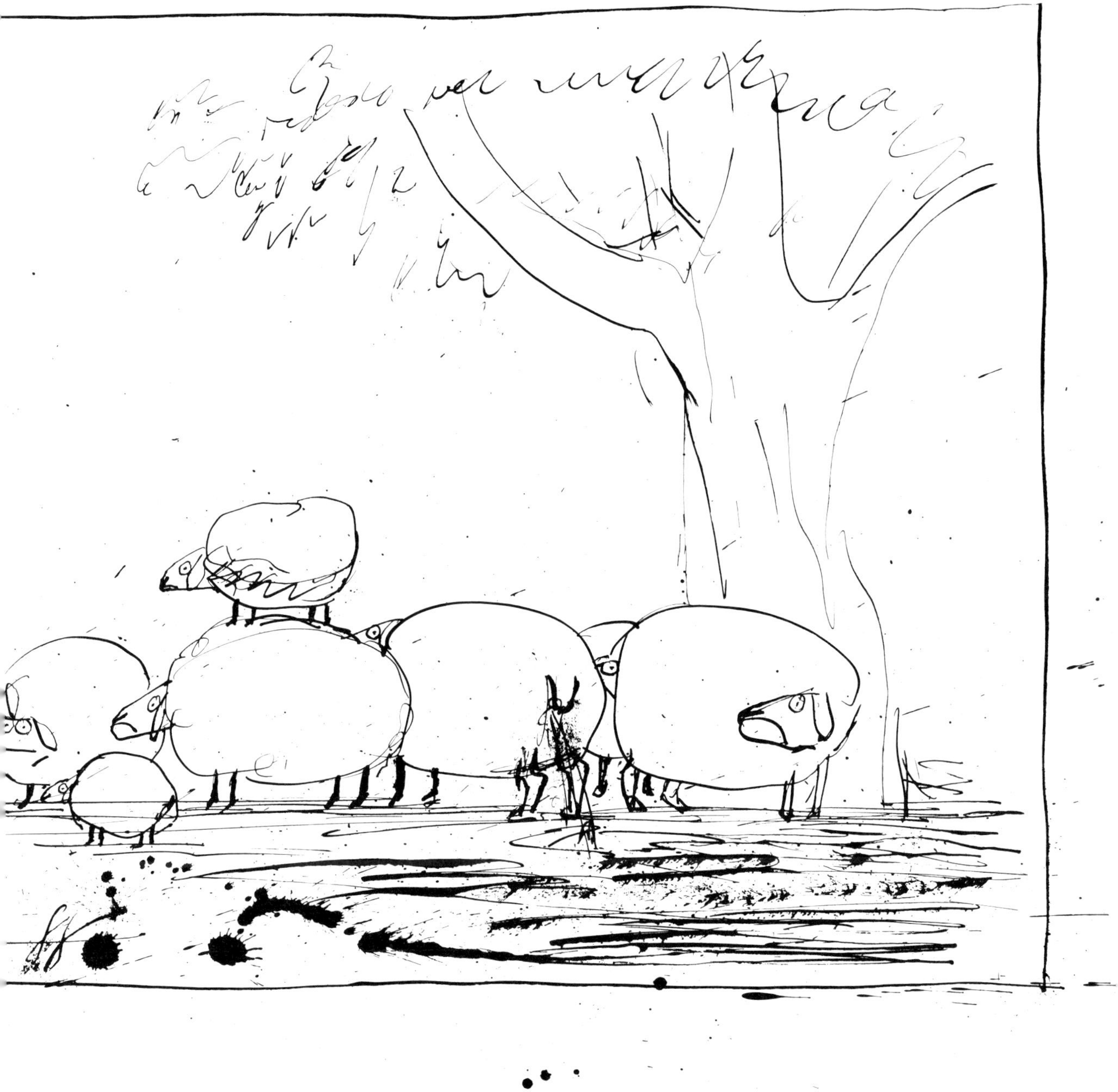

FLOP
TRIES TO
SMILE.

REGAL FLOP.

THE PUZZLED ALERT.

CERTAIN GUILT.

TWO FACED FLOP.

THE BACK PEDDLE.

FLOP NEEDS A BATH

MEALTIME.

BORED ACQUIESCENCE

CAT!

WET DAY

THE EMBARRASSED NECK STRETCH.

THE FLOOR SLIDE.

INNOCENT.

CRINGING DECEIT.

WHERE HAVE YOU BEEN, FLOP?

FLOP ADOPTS THE SINGING POSITION
WHEN I PLAY THE TRUMPET

THE FLOP SMILE

THE DOORBELL!

FLOP ON THE FLOOR

FEAR

RELUCTANCE.

DISTRUST.

THE STRETCH POSITION.

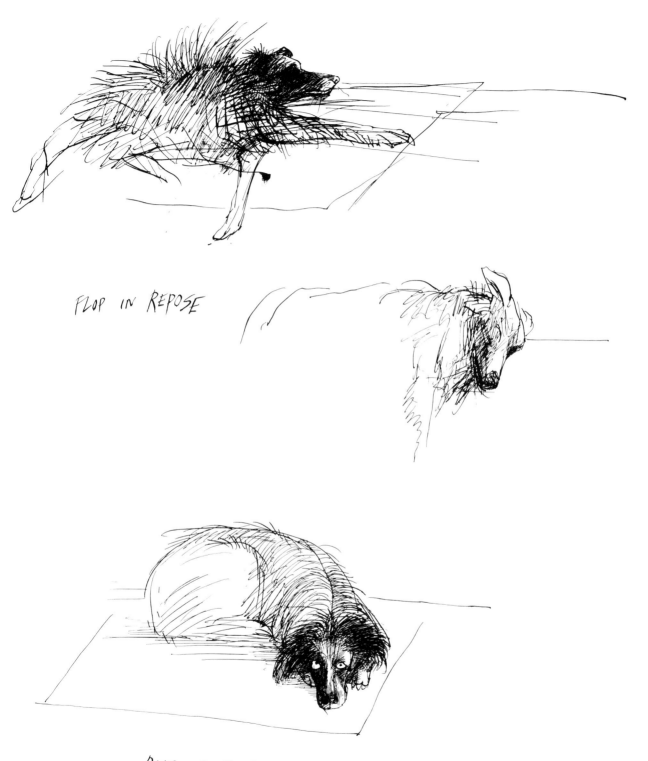

FLOP IN REPOSE

DOUBTING FLOP.

Record of an unfortunate correspondence
between FLOP'S master and the
Post Office

DOG LOOSE 151410 11-5-89
12.30

DOG LOOSE 151410 11-5-89
12.30

Ralph Steadman

DOG LOOSE 151410 11-5-89

Mr & Mrs

Old

15 9SE,

Royal Mail Letters
A part of The Post Office

D Blake
District Head Postmaster

Military Road
CANTERBURY
CT1 1AA

Telephone
Canterbury (0227) 475 232
Extension

Girobank account 315 9590

date · 12 January 1989
your ref
our ref 637/889 RSW/HM

Mr Steadman

Dear Sir

It has been reported that Mr. W.Howard, a postman attached to the Maidstone
Office, while on duty at Old Drive at about 0900 on the 31 December 1988 was
bitten by a dog, of which you are understood to be the owner. The local
police have been notified of the incident.

I must ask you to have the dog kept under control to ensure that it cannot
mennace or attack Post Office staff at times when postal deliveries are
being made.

I am to add that unless the dog is kept under control it will not be possible
to continue delivery at your premises.

Yours faithfully

R S WOOD ·

Dear Sir,

I am in receipt of your letter 12th January 1989 concerning the alleged behaviour of my dog towards one of your postmen.

It is a distressing situation and I trust that the postman concerned was not seriously injured. Could I enquire as to whether he received a proper bite, or was it, as is normal with my dog, a warning nip around the ankles similar to the kind she gives whilst rounding up the sheep ?

Though this does not diminish my concern, I suspect the latter was the case. It is a common trait in the Border Collie breed. It has often crossed my mind that if I had bitten the postman, I could tell you why I did it, but unfortunately I cannot tell you why a dog decides to go for some people rather than others. Ironically, she always tends to adopt such tactics with those visitors who we are genuinely pleased to see and we cannot praise your services to us over the years too highly.

However, because I am so concerned I have consulted a dog psychiatrist, Mr. Peter Neville, who claims he can cure our dog of the habit with the aid of a rape alarm set off by me at the first sign of an 'attack' and before a nip might occur. This serves to divert the dog's attention and, according to Mr. Neville, makes it think twice about its behaviour. We shall see.

Our first test will take place with the help of our milkman whose moving float is also a common target. He will act as guinea pig. I should then be obliged if one of your postmen of a less nervous disposition can be forewarned that such a test is imminent. Rape alarms are noted for their piercing scream.

Please, be assured that every reasonable attempt will be made to 'cure' my dog.

Yours faithfully,

Ralph Steadman.